Crocodile Attack

Leone Peguero
Illustrated by Liz Wilks

**Peta-Lynn Mann was twelve years old
when her friend, Hilton Graham,
was attacked by a large crocodile.
It was 1981 and they were boating at
Channel Point near Darwin in the
Northern Territory of Australia.
This is her story of bravery and courage.**

TRUE STORIES
OF BRAVERY & COURAGE

**BRAVE
KIDS**

BlueCatBooks

First published in 2004, Reprint 2004
BlueCatBooks
PO Box 3006
Eltham VIC 3095
Australia

email: peguero@bigpond.net.au
website: www.bluecatbooks.com.au

National Library of Australia
Cataloguing-in-Publication entry:
        Peguero, Leone.
        Crocodile attack: true stories of bravery and courage.

        For children aged 8+.
        ISBN 0 9578422 4 4.

        1. Crocodiles - Juvenile literature. 2. Heroes - Juvenile
        literature. 3. Courage - Juvenile literature. I. Wilks,
        Liz. II. Title. (Series: Brave kids; book one).

        179.6

Book & cover design by Lee Lewis
Printed in Australia by McPherson's Printing Group

Distributed nationally and in New Zealand
by Dennis Jones & Associates

WHAT WOULD YOU DO?

A large crocodile is attacking your friend.
A raging boar is savaging your dad.
Your friends have drifted a long way
from land in rough seas.

How can any of us be sure what we would do
if faced with such dilemmas?

We do know, however, that the children in these
stories decided to place themselves
in just that kind of danger to save someone
else's life.

**Each of the stories in the series BRAVE KIDS
is based on a true incident of bravery.
While some details have been
added, the basic stories have been
confirmed from available records.**

*TRUE STORIES
OF BRAVERY & COURAGE* **BRAVE KIDS**

Acknowledgements

Thanks are due to the Royal Humane Society of Australasia for allowing us to use a representation of the Clarke Gold Medal and for kindly providing relevant information. Also thank you to Adam Deverell for his contribution to research; to Helen Katz for making time in her busy schedule to cast her keen eye over work in progress; to Liz Wilks for contributing over and beyond the call of duty; and to Althea Brooks for her unflagging assistance throughout all stages of the project.

Contents

PAPUA
NEW
GUINEA

SOLOMON
ISLANDS

NORTHERN
TERRITORY

AUSTRALIA

FIJI

NEW ZEALAND

MAP KEY
For story events and
recorded instances of
crocodile attack

1 **Darwin**
2 **Channel Point**
3 **Sweet's Lookout**
4 **Roper River**
5 **Pindi Pindi**
6 **Townsville**
7 **Barron River**
8 **Kakadu National Park**
9 **Johnston River**
10 **Cairns**
11 **Port Douglas**
12 **Kimberley Coast**
13 **East Alligator River**
14 **Prince Regent River**

Wetlands are also known around the world as swamp, marsh and bog. They are home to many plants, animals and migratory birds.

The Top End is the name commonly given to the northern part of Australia taking in the three states of the Northern Territory, Queensland and Western Australia. There are two main seasons in this area.

The wet in the Top End of Australia is typically from October to April. It brings heavy rain and heat. Animals give birth and the swamps and rivers are full of food.

The dry is the name often given to the rest of the year. This is when the country is prone to bushfires and drought. Food is scarce and the creeks and rivers dry up.

1 The Promise

Peta-Lynn was glad to be home from boarding school. She was going to spend Easter on an adventure holiday with Nimrod Safari.

This business was run by her parents and their business partner, Hilton Graham. They took tourists around the Top End of Australia. Another tour was about to begin and Peta was going too.

They were to travel down to the safari camp at Channel Point where the tour would begin. Hilton had promised to take Peta with him in the jeep. They planned to arrive first and have the whole of

the first day to explore the wetlands on the safari airboat.

Peta's dad was to bring the bus and the tourist guests the next day.

It was the wet season so there would be plenty of animals and birds to see. And that included crocodiles.

No wonder Peta was keen to get going.

Crocodiles are reptiles that live both on land and in water.
There are 23 species of crocodile left in the world.
Like other reptiles, they breathe air and are 'cold-blooded'. This means they need to warm themselves by lying in the sun.
To cool down, they lie in the shade with their mouths wide open, or laze in the water.
Crocodiles have at least 60 teeth. These are large and sharp for catching and holding onto prey, but not suitable for chewing. Instead they tear up their prey and spend long stretches of time digesting it.
Some species can live up to 70 years.

Alligator

Alligators are closely related to crocodiles and often confused with them.
The alligator's snout is 'U-shaped'. When an alligator closes its mouth, you can't see its lower teeth. Its thick bumpy skin is darker than a croc's.
There are no wild alligators in Australia.

The crocodile's skull and jaws are longer and narrower than the alligator's. Its snout is 'V-shaped'. When a crocodile closes its mouth you can see *all* of its teeth.

Saltwater crocodile

The saltwater crocodile is the largest of the two species of crocodile found in Australia. These crocs are often called 'salties'.

They not only swim in the ocean, but also in rivers and billabongs. That means they can live in both saltwater and freshwater.

Salties can grow to over six metres in length and are usually around 400 - 500 kilos.

The saltwater crocodile has a broad, powerful snout and an uneven jawline with teeth of varying size.

Freshwater crocodile

The freshwater crocodile is the second of the two species found in Australia. It lives only in the freshwater of rivers and billabongs.

It has quite a long, smooth and slender snout with a straight jawline.

All its teeth are nearly equal in size.

Males may reach up to three metres in length.

Females are smaller at around two metres.

They can take up to 30 years to reach their maximum size.

2 To the Wetlands

Peta and Hilton were on their way to the safari camp. Familiar landscape whizzed by the window.

As usual, Hilton had packed his revolver.

'Are we going to hunt as well as explore today?' Peta asked.

'Sure,' replied Hilton. 'We need something large and juicy for tomorrow's barbecue.'

It was the wet season so Peta knew there would be heaps of game around. 'Wild pig?' she guessed.

Hilton nodded.

Certainly not crocodile. They had been protected in Australia since the late 1960s. That means hunting crocodiles is against the law.

'Got to have something to show those tourists,' Peta's dad always said with a laugh. The excitement of seeing crocodiles was good for business.

Darter

Tourism was only part of the story. Crocodiles had been in the sea, lakes and rivers since the days of the dinosaurs. Now that's a long time! What right did humans have to kill every one of them?

Peta sat back as the jeep roared its way to Channel Point.

Crocodiles were part of the way of life in the Top End of Australia. But not everyone felt happy about that.

The local newspaper that Hilton had tossed in with their luggage often carried articles on issues concerning crocodiles.

 Every year, hundreds of crocodiles are removed from Darwin Bay. Usually these crocs are taken to a crocodile farm. These farms have been permitted to breed crocodiles for commercial purposes.

Any crocodile captured in the wild, for safety reasons, may also be taken to a crocodile farm.

 We should remember that more people die each year from causes such as lightning strike or bee sting than crocodile attack. While the possibility of a crocodile attack can excite the human imagination, it doesn't bring about the death of large numbers of people.

3 Croc Trouble

Dear Sir,

We have been told that crocodiles must be respected as an endangered species. That's all very well, but where do people fit into this picture?

I've always walked my dogs around the rocks at Darwin Bay. But now the croc problem is so bad I will have to give it up. One of my dogs has already been killed. I've no doubt it was taken by a croc.

First there were small ones lurking out in the waters. Now they are up to four metres long. And I'm not the only one to have seen them. The local fishermen reckon there are now more crocs in Darwin than down south in the wild.

The fishermen say they are not so worried about the crocs in the sea because they can keep an eye on them. It's the crocs in the billabongs and swamps that are the worry.

Well, I'm worried enough about those in the bay. They are definitely dangerous animals. How long do we all have to put up with this menace?

Scott Midler

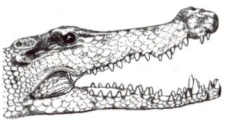

Dear Sir,

I understand Scott Midler's feelings about the crocs in our area, but he has to remember how all this began. Saltwater crocodiles in the Top End of Australia were once hunted and shot almost out of existence.

One hundred years ago crocodile shooting was a major industry. The skins and meat of crocodiles were worth a lot of money. Then in the late 1960s and early 1970s they were declared a protected species.

Over the next decade the crocodile population made a remarkable recovery.

There should be no question of their right to continue to live here. They have been a part of the land for thousands of years. It just requires us to take extra care to be able to live with them.

And it is worth it for many reasons. Remember, farming crocodiles in large numbers for meat and skin products is now allowed. They also attract tourists, who are vital to the survival of local business.

When you add it all up, the crocodile brings many more benefits than problems.

Dr John Sheenan

'Do you think we'll see any crocs today?' Peta asked. 'How about one as big as Sweetheart?'

Hilton laughed. 'I certainly hope not. That was one big croc.'

The Story of Sweetheart

Crocodiles do not usually attack boats but the crocodile that was to become known as Sweetheart did.

Maybe he was upset by the noise that boats made in his peaceful billabong. Or he may have mistaken the boats for other crocs. Whatever the cause, like Moby Dick, the great white whale, he would come straight at a craft and crash right into it.

The first attack was in 1974 at Sweet's Lookout Billabong on the Finniss River.

Three people were fishing from a boat at night when the crocodile surfaced, grabbed the cowling of the outboard motor and shook the boat violently. One person was thrown out, but managed to scramble back in.

It was time to escape! But the crocodile struck again. This time it was the propeller.

In 1976, there was a similar boat attack. This time the crocodile damaged the cowling and punctured the aluminium hull. That same year, a crocodile slammed into a fishing boat from underneath,

turning it around before surfacing alongside. It was thought to be Sweetheart.

In 1978, a moored boat was attacked and the outboard engine damaged. Also, another fishing boat was attacked and sunk.

Not surprisingly, everyone became afraid to go near the billabong. So in 1979, just before a fishing competition was to be held nearby, a large hunt was carried out and a big croc was captured.

Some say that Sweetheart became entangled in a trap and drowned.

Others say that the stress, after its capture, killed the big croc.

And still others believe that the wrong croc was captured and the real Sweetheart still swims those waters.

The body and skeleton of the crocodile known as Sweetheart can be seen at the Darwin Museum.

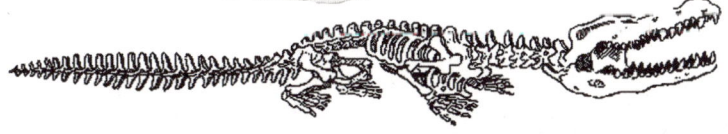

'I wonder if they really captured Sweetheart,' Peta said.

'Must have been him,' said Hilton. 'Those kind of attacks have stopped.'

'But we can't be sure,' said Peta quickly. 'There was more than one large croc in that billabong.'

She liked to think that Sweetheart was still out there somewhere. He had a right to be, rather than on display at the museum in Darwin, even if those exhibits did attract large numbers of tourists each year.

'He lived in his billabong a long time before motorboats started to annoy him,' said Peta.

Crocodiles evolved about 200 million years ago. They lived at the same time as the dinosaurs and probably ate some of them. They have survived for all that time as a top predator.

Crocodiles have such excellent senses they are able to hunt by stealth. Their eyesight is as good as ours, and even better under water. Their sense of hearing is acute. This makes for an excellent hunter.

They feed on animals ranging from insects and frogs to fish, turtles and birds. Large crocodiles will attack animals as large as a fully-grown buffalo.

Hilton agreed. 'Probably well over fifty years.'

'And he never did hurt anyone,' added Peta.

Hilton smiled. 'Seemed he just got to be one cranky croc whenever a noisy motorboat disturbed his peace and quiet.'

Peta closed her eyes and leant back and dozed. It was time to forget about large crocs for the moment.

 Baru is the name given to the saltwater crocodile by the Gumatj people of the north eastern coastal region of the Northern Territory. They are also known as the saltwater or crocodile people.

Most coastal aborigines regard the crocodile as a sacred animal and an important part of their way of life and culture. This is expressed in crocodile dreaming: stories, songs and dances about the crocodile.

Within many aboriginal communities the crocodile cannot be hunted. For thousands of years they have followed this law. To look after the crocodile means to look after their country as their ancestors did.

4 Safari Camp

T he city bustle had been left far behind. Magpie geese flew overhead as Peta and Hilton drove through the shimmering wetlands.

'Awake again?' said Hilton.

The earliest record of a crocodile attack was in 1870. A man was taken at Roper River in the Northern Territory while he was asleep in a boat with one of his legs hanging over into the river.

Two schoolgirls disappeared as they rode their horses to school at Pindi Pindi, Queensland in 1933. One girl was drowned. The body of the other girl was found in a crocodile's stomach.

They were now driving along the narrow road close to the safari camp at Channel Point. As soon as they arrived, there would be jobs to do before they could go exploring on the water.

'Don't worry,' Hilton said, 'we'll get going soon.'

Peta would have loved to have taken a long cool swim straight away. But that wasn't an option. There were too many stories of what could happen when people failed to take care around crocodiles.

In 1954 the Clarke Silver Medal was awarded by the Royal Humane Society of Australasia to Clifford Robinson, a zoo manager, in Townsville, Queensland. The award was for attempting to rescue Hughie Henry, from a crocodile at Mount St John Zoo, on 22 September 1953.

Hughie Henry was attacked when he entered an enclosure that contained four large crocodiles. His cries were heard by Mrs Robinson, who called her husband. Clifford Robinson drove to the pool and attacked the crocodile with a wooden paling. But the crocodile dragged Hughie under the water. Mr Robinson held onto Hughie and tried to pull him clear. However, the crocodile held fast. Mr Robinson found a reaping hook nearby and gave it to Hughie, who then attacked the crocodile with it.

Mr Robinson again left the water and went for a rifle. When he returned, the crocodile had released Hughie and disappeared.

Mr Robinson immediately entered the water and brought Hughie to the bank. Unfortunately, he had already died from his wounds.

Taking care was certainly what Peta and Hilton planned to do.

Tourist operators, who run crocodile-spotting cruises, think that crocodiles should stay free in the wild. They also believe that people can live with crocodiles safely if they take the right precautions.

 Never swim in the water, especially at night.

 Don't go near crocodile nesting grounds.

 Camp well away from water.

 Back away quietly from basking crocs.

 Do not get between water and a crocodile.

5 Wild Pig Hunt

At last Peta's trip through the wetlands had begun. Hilton steered the boat while Peta sat back. This was fun.

'There should be plenty of pigs around here,' Hilton said. 'Keep your eyes open.'

James Mason was ten years old when in 1983 he and his father and brother went swimming in the Barron River, Queensland. They were in shallow muddy water when, without warning, a splash was heard and the father turned to find he could not see his eldest boy, Jimmy, anywhere. He threw the other child on the bank and dived into the water. He found the boy and grabbed onto his legs.

Jimmy, however, was pulled away from his father and, soon after, the crocodile rose in the middle of the river with one of the child's legs in its mouth.

Waterfowl stood in the shallows and stared at the noisy boat as it hummed past them.

It was another hot day and very humid, but Peta didn't mind. She had been looking forward to this trip for some time.

Wild boar

Although they went quite a distance, they didn't see any wild pigs, so Hilton turned the boat around and headed back to camp. To be safe, he kept the boat near the edge of the swamp.

It was then they came to a sudden and violent stop. Hilton fell forward and Peta had to hold on to the side of the boat to save herself from falling into the water.

'What's happened?' she cried.

'We've grounded in the mud,' said Hilton and jumped over the side of the boat. The water only reached his knees. He needed to push the boat back into deeper water and be quick about it.

But it wasn't going to be so simple. As he bent forward to push, Hilton's pistol slid from its holster into the water.

Magpie geese

In 1985, during a midnight swim in the Daintree River in the far north of Queensland, a Christmas party ended tragically when a local shopkeeper, Beryl Wruck, decided to cool off in the water.

Mrs Wruck, the mother of three children, disappeared as she crouched in the shallows.

According to one of the other swimmers that night, there was a huge swirl and he was pushed aside. Beryl went up in the air and over and then she was gone. There was no sound, no scream. It all happened very quickly.

Daintree people knew that crocodiles had been seen in the creek, but they thought they would be safe at low tide, when the water was shallow.

It is thought that the attack was a typical crocodile ambush. Beryl, crouched down in the water, appeared to be small prey for the saltwater croc.

Fingernails, toenails, and what were assumed to be Mrs Wruck's bones, were found several weeks later in a large, trapped crocodile.

6 The Silent Killer

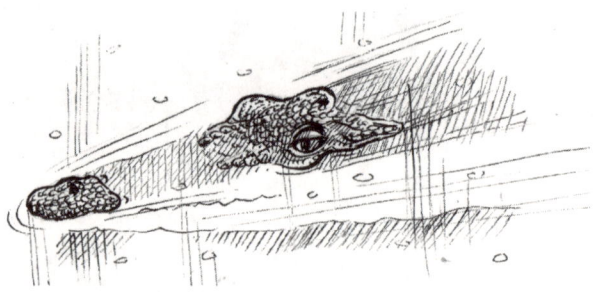

Everything began to happen so quickly that Peta didn't even have time to scream.

One second Hilton was standing in the water, the next he was slammed into the side of the boat with tremendous force. A crocodile's ferocious teeth and snapping jaws were coming straight towards him.

Hilton put his left arm up to protect his face.

The crocodile is often described as 'the silent killer'. No wonder. Attacks happen at amazing speed. Eyewitnesses often say that they hardly saw or heard anything. Not only are the attacks fast, crocodiles can surge a full body length out of the water.

The huge jaws clamped shut on his raised arm and forced Hilton to his knees. Then the crocodile began to drag him away from the boat and into deeper water.

Peta jumped out of the boat and ran through the shallow water towards the river bank. She had to get away from the crocodile. She had to get away to where she would be safe. Away from the ferocious jaws and from the blood and the screaming.

In 1994, a group of tourists were present when a large crocodile killed its handler at the Johnston River Crocodile Farm in North Queensland.

The handler, who had two years of experience with crocodiles, was inside the crocodile enclosure. While tourists looked on, he tapped the crocodile with a rake. The crocodile, just over four metres long, attacked, striking him on the upper arm and dragging him into the water. The crocodile rolled with the man's head and arm in its jaws.

One tourist seized a pole and hit at the crocodile. Another grabbed hold of one of the man's ankles and tried to pull him away.

The rescue attempt was unsuccessful.

A teenage girl was mauled by a crocodile close to the city centre in Cairns, Queensland while swimming in a creek. The crocodile grabbed one of her legs and dragged her under the water. Two friends heard screams and raced to help. One young man climbed onto a branch and pulled the girl up by her hair. He passed her to the other man who had waded into the creek. The first man then yelled and splashed to distract the crocodile. The bleeding girl was finally hauled from the water.

A girl survived an attack by a saltwater crocodile at Port Douglas, Queensland in 2001. Taleesha Fagatilli was playing in the water when the large crocodile struck and dragged her into deeper water where it began a death roll. The croc then released eight-year-old Taleesha, who swam to safety. She was rushed to hospital where she had emergency surgery for deep bites and cuts to her chest, leg and arm.

A group of tourists entered the water at Sandy Billabong, Kakadu National Park, during October 2002, close to midnight. The group were swimming some distance from shore when one of them felt something bump his leg. He then saw a large dark shape take the woman next to him under the water. The woman's body was later found two kilometres from the attack site.

Jacana (Lily trotter)

 # 7 The Moment

Peta stood on the bank not far from where Hilton was being dragged by the large crocodile into deep water.

Hilton looked towards her and stretched out his hand. He needed help to fight off the attack.

Peta would have been safe on the bank. She could have stayed there, huddled amongst the paperbark trees, away from the jaws of the crocodile. But could she ignore her friend's plea?

'How can I fight a crocodile?' thought Peta, as she watched the terrible scene before her.

Hilton was kicking the crocodile and punching it with his one free hand, as it thrashed and pulled at his body.

Then Peta made her decision.

She jumped into the water and grabbed onto Hilton. She was so close to the crocodile she could almost touch its bumpy, scaly skin and see into its golden eyes.

Now she too was being pulled away into even deeper water. Still she clung to her friend with all her strength.

 A crocodile will often roll when it has large prey in its jaws. By rolling under the water it can stop the fight by drowning its prey. This is often referred to as a **death roll**.

 It has been said by some, who have lived to tell the tale, that a crocodile's breath is putrid. Also, its groan can make the hair stand up on the back of your neck. Best to believe these people, rather than try to find out for ourselves!

At last the crocodile let go and disappeared into the water. Hilton's arm was badly broken, but he was free of those jaws.

'What,' Peta wondered, 'should they do now?'

The boat was too far from them to reach.

They were forced to turn towards the bank and scramble through the reeds to safety.

Peta jumped up on the bank again and reached back to help Hilton up. Surely they could get away now.

But the crocodile wasn't finished with them yet.

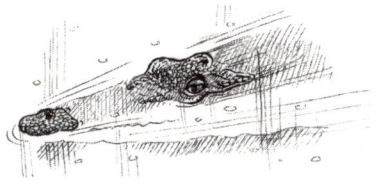

8 Death Roll

The crocodile came to the surface, swimming fast with jaws wide open. Its powerful tail was thrusting its giant body forward.

It leapt from the water. Its jaws fastened onto Hilton's thigh, ripping him away from Peta's hands.

The crocodile held Hilton fast. This time he could not fight back.

Peta acted quickly. Again she grabbed Hilton by his uninjured arm. Letting herself sink into the muddy bank, she stuck in her heels and leaned back, putting all her weight into her legs.

But the crocodile half dragged, half carried them into the water.

Now both Peta and Hilton were at its mercy. It was then that the crocodile rolled, taking them into even deeper water. All three went under.

Somehow Peta regained her footing. She did not let go of Hilton. Instead she pulled with all her strength and his head finally reappeared.

But so did the croc's!

Still Peta did not let go. Terrified and sobbing, she held on.

She could see the pain Hilton was in, but he didn't let go of her hand. Desperately she began to pull him away from the sharp, bloodstained teeth of the crocodile.

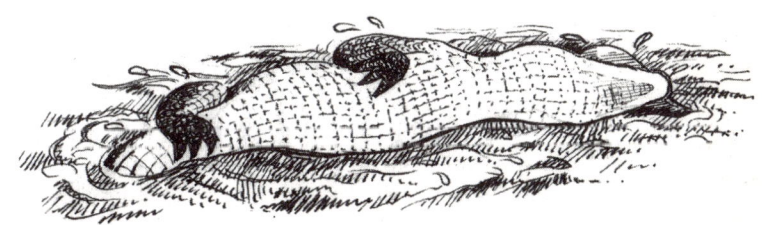

Death roll

Perhaps the crocodile was unable to manoeuvre properly against the extra weight of both of them. It let go.

It was a struggle for Peta to pull Hilton up the bank. He was so heavy. But she had to try. He was too weak from fighting the crocodile to climb up by himself.

Val Plumwood was on a lone canoeing expedition through flooded waters in the Kakadu National Park when she saw what she thought was a floating log. Edging in for a closer look, Ms Plumwood realised it was a crocodile, then could not back off in time.

The crocodile began attacking the canoe and followed her as she paddled away.

Fearing that she would be thrown into the water, she tried to reach the edge of the swamp by grasping some overhanging branches.

As she did so, she was seized and pulled into the water. The crocodile then spun her around and her face came back to the surface.

By death rolling, the crocodile had begun to lose its grip. Ms Plumwood was able to break away again, swim behind a paperbark tree and start to climb it.

The crocodile struck again and she flung herself onto a steep, muddy bank. At first she was unable to climb it, slipping back again and again towards the waiting crocodile. Eventually she found that if she spread her fingers and dug them into the mud, she could haul herself up and away from the crocodile.

Blood pumped from her torn thighs and buttocks. Tearing off strips of her clothing to make bandages, she began the agonising struggle through the bushland to reach the park rangers' station.

Some hours later, the rangers found her. Concerned by her failure to return, they had started a search.

It took all night, and relays of boats and vehicles, to move Ms Plumwood from the flooded park. After emergency surgery at Darwin Hospital and further operations in Sydney, she made a good recovery.

9 Terrible Tug of War

Once again the crocodile attacked. This time it grabbed Hilton's buttock. Still Peta held tightly to her friend. The battle had become a terrible tug of war to save Hilton's life.

Then, just as Peta thought she couldn't hold on any longer, the crocodile loosened its grip on Hilton. His feet fell onto the bank and the crocodile sank back into the water.

Before it could attack again, Peta pulled Hilton as hard as she could up onto the bank.

For an awful moment Peta thought the crocodile

would try and climb up after them.

As Peta helped Hilton, she looked back fearfully at the crocodile. But it didn't move. It just followed them with its eyes.

Hilton could hardly walk and was only partly conscious. It had taken all his strength to get away. His pants were torn and blood soaked. His flesh hung loosely from his thigh.

Clearly the crocodile had done a lot of damage.

 The future of the crocodile in Australia and Papua New Guinea has been assured through protection and management programs. However, in many other parts of the world their numbers are decreasing rapidly.

 In Papua New Guinea, programs are in place to make sure that the crocodile population is kept stable. The management system involves a combination of wild cropping, egg and hatchling harvest, and farming.

10 Race Against Time

When Peta looked back again at the swamp, she couldn't see the crocodile.

The safari camp was some distance from the swamp down a bush track. Normally this was a good thing, because it kept plenty of distance between animals and people. But today it added another difficulty.

Hilton couldn't walk that far, nor could he walk

as far as the parked jeep.

Peta saw that Hilton's face had turned white and he had started to shake. It was the shock of the attack.

For the first time Peta realised that Hilton could die. His battle with the crocodile had been nightmare enough, but the fight was far from over.

How could this have happened?

Maybe those people who said the problem with the crocs had got out of hand were right.

Peta knew that crocodiles were an important part of her family's business. Many of the tourists who joined their safari trips were keen to see them.

Yet here she was, because of a ferocious crocodile attack, racing against time to save her friend's life.

Hilton was too big for her to support all the way to the camp. There was only one thing for her to do. She would have to drive the jeep to Hilton.

This meant leaving him while she went to get it.

Water buffalo

Peta ran back to the parked jeep. She had to find the strength to get Hilton to hospital and the help he needed.

The key was in the jeep's ignition. Peta looked at it grimly and thought, 'I'm not sure I can do this.'

She had been taught to drive, but it wasn't as if she had practised often. In fact, it was Hilton who had taught her when she was just nine. Now she hoped those skills would help to save him.

She started the jeep, pushing the clutch in tightly. The engine chugged and spluttered. She revved the accelerator and tried to put it into first gear. But it just made a terrible noise.

She tried again. This time she got it into gear and the jeep lurched forward onto the dirt road.

This was scary but she had to make it.

A young boy fought his way out of the jaws of a three-metre crocodile by gouging its eyes. The saltwater croc had attacked Sam West as he snorkelled off Western Australia's Kimberley coast. His father, a prawn trawler owner, later said that the crocodile had gripped his son's head, released him, then gripped his hands. In all it struck four or five times. Mr West was proud of his son's courage in fighting back by gouging the croc's eyes. Sam suffered cuts to the head, wrists and hands. Later, a zoologist said eye gouging was probably the only chance of fending off such a large crocodile as its body is so well armoured.

A local man slipped and fell while fishing on a concrete bridge across the East Alligator River. A large crocodile was known to swim in the area. Witnesses saw the man try to swim to safety, but the crocodile took him by the head and swam away with him.

His body was later recovered; however, the capture of the crocodile was prevented by local aborigines, who regard the crocodile as a totem and therefore sacred to them.

Note: When early European settlers came to this area, they tended to use the word 'alligator' or 'gator' instead of the correct description of 'crocodile'. This led to place names such as the East Alligator River.

Tree frog

11 Call for Help

After a bumpy ride, Peta managed to drive back to Hilton. He had hobbled about 400 metres towards camp by the time she got to him.

'We've got to get you into the jeep, and back to camp,' she told him.

Hilton nodded. That was where the first aid equipment was kept.

Despite his injuries, Hilton climbed into the jeep and Peta drove back to camp.

Crocodile wounds are dangerous because they become infected quickly. Before Peta could even think of driving Hilton to hospital she had to stop

41

the bleeding and clean the wounds as best she could.

She began at once. Luckily, her dad had taught her first aid. 'When you're in the bush,' he had told her, 'you have to help yourself.'

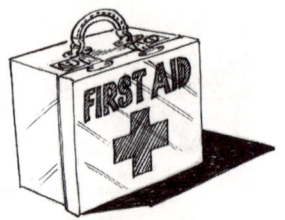

Peta sterilised Hilton's wounds with antiseptic, which made him wince in pain. Then she wrapped his arm and leg tightly in bandages.

Next she collected the CB radio, which was kept on the front dashboard. Hilton and her dad kept in contact with the CB, as there were no phones in the bush and no mobile telephones at that time. Peta supported Hilton as he called for help.

'This is Channel Point Camp, does anyone have a copy? This is an emergency. Over. Over.'

There was silence apart from the crackling of the radio.

Hilton repeated the message several times.

At last there came a welcome voice. 'This is Labell Camp, I have a copy. Go ahead Channel Camp.'

'It's an emergency! There's been a crocodile

attack! We need help.'

'Channel Camp, we'll send a rescue party right away.'

That was good news, but waiting for Labell Camp would waste valuable time, Peta decided. Hilton's arm was badly broken and his thigh wounds were deep. And he had lost a lot of blood.

It would be better to drive out of camp and meet them along the way. They told the man on the CB their plan.

'Roger, Channel Camp,' he said. 'Over.'

At this stage, no one had any idea that they were relying on a young girl to drive the injured man to safety.

 Health researchers are keen to find out more about the bacteria on a crocodile's teeth. It seems crocodiles, unlike humans and other animals, are immune to the bacteria, melioidosis, which is found in tropical soils and has caused several human deaths over the years. They believe that something in crocodile blood may have important antibacterial properties.

Crocodile bite wounds have caused extreme discomfort and have healed slowly because of the presence of this bacteria.

12 Croc Attack

18 April 1981

Hilton Graham, of Nimrod Safari, was rushed to Darwin's Casuarina Hospital by road yesterday and admitted to the Emergency Department, having been severely mauled by a large crocodile at Channel Point.

Following surgery, he is now recovering and his condition today is reported as satisfactory.

He has a broken left forearm, received when fighting off the crocodile, and extensive cuts to one thigh.

It appears that Mr Hilton entered the water to free the boat he was travelling in from an embankment. A large male crocodile then attacked.

Conservation officers are to travel to the area today to investigate the scene of the attack.

Imagine the surprise of the rescue party when they met up with the jeep on the track. That's when they found a young girl had helped fight off a crocodile and driven her badly injured friend to safety.

Best of all, Hilton was going to recover. Peta had done all she possibly could to save him. It would take long, slow months before his wounds were completely healed, but he had survived. And

he wouldn't give up on crocodiles. In fact, Hilton Graham went on to become a crocodile farmer!

No wonder Peta's parents were proud of her. She had shown tremendous bravery in the face of very real danger.

Soon after, a search of the wetlands was made by staff of a nearby camp site. The safari airboat was found several metres from land. During this search a crocodile aggressively approached the boat. A shot was fired at it and, though thrashing and bubbling was seen, the crocodile disappeared.

Wildlife rangers checked the area thoroughly, but found no sign of the croc, dead or alive.

When news of the rescue and of the young girl's courage became known, everyone was amazed.

Who could be sure that they would have done the same in her place?

Bravery Awards

The Royal Humane Society of Australasia recognises, through a number of awards, acts of bravery by those who risk their own lives in saving, or attempting to save, the lives of others.

The Clarke Gold Medal is the highest award of the Society. It is awarded for the most outstanding case of bravery considered during the year in Australia. Very few have been awarded.

The Rupert Wilks Trophy is only awarded to a child under the age of thirteen at the time of a brave act or rescue.

Peta's Awards

TRUE STORIES OF BRAVERY & COURAGE

BRAVE KIDS

Peta-Lynn Mann received two bravery awards for the courage she showed in rescuing Hilton Graham from a crocodile attack. The awards were presented by the Queen during a state visit in 1982.

Only two people have ever been awarded both the Clarke Gold Medal and the Rupert Wilks Trophy. One of the award winners was 12-year-old Peta-Lynn Mann from Darwin, in the Northern Territory of Australia.

Not all acts of bravery are awarded in this way but, when they are, they can serve as a reminder of how we rely on each other.

We are also reminded that children can do brave things too.